Mindful Meditation

30 Days Uniting with the Heart of God

Jeanie Winebarger

Copyright © 2018 Jeanie Winebarger

All rights reserved. No part of this collection may be reproduced or transmitted in any form or by any means, electronic or mechanical, including photocopying and recording, or by any information storage and retrieval system, except in the case of brief quotations for use in articles and reviews, without written permission from the author.

7710-T Cherry Park Dr, Ste 224

Houston, TX 77095

713-766-4271

ISBN: 978-1-68411-591-4

Contents

Acknowledgments v
Introduction vii
Daily Call: Day 1 1
Daily Call: Day 2 3
Daily Call: Day 3 7
Daily Call: Day 4 9
Daily Call: Day 5 11
Daily Call: Day 6 15
Daily Call: Day 7 19
Daily Call: Day 8 23
Daily Call: Day 9 27
Daily Call: Day 10 29
Daily Call: Day 11 33
Daily Call: Day 12 37
Daily Call: Day 13 39
Daily Call: Day 14 43
Daily Call: Day 15 47
Daily Call: Day 16 49
Daily Call: Day 17 53
Daily Call: Day 18 57
Daily Call: Day 19 61
Daily Call: Day 20 63
Daily Call: Day 21 65
Daily Call: Day 22 69
Daily Call: Day 23 73

Daily Call: Day 24 77
Daily Call: Day 25 81
Daily Call: Day 26 83
Daily Call: Day 27 87
Daily Call: Day 28 91
Daily Call: Day 29 93
Daily Call: Day 30 95
NOTES 97
About the Author 101

Acknowledgments

I want to thank my husband, Don, for supporting me in my journey to help others. He has allowed me to spend countless hours away from him as I wrote and rewrote. He encouraged me each step and graciously gave me feedback on content.

My sister-in-law, Wanda Counts, spent time with me in the editing and rewriting process. My cousin Sylvia Gunter, who is an author and publisher, encouraged me and gave me her opinions based on her own experiences.

My publisher, Eddie Smith, author and speaker, stood quietly in the background. He gently and gingerly led me toward a better-finished product, yet never interfered with my vision and content. He allowed me to be me.

I am also thankful for you, Dear Reader, for daring to take this challenge. I know God speaks and believe He is whispering your name right now.

Introduction

Everyone today is searching for peace. Our hearts are unsettled. Our bodies are in constant motion, pretending we can meet every demand that is screaming simultaneously from every direction. Moment to moment our mind is swept away with another thought like the grains of sand tossed about by the waves on a stormy beach. Inertia sets in. A body in motion tends to stay in motion. We can't stop the madness. We are afraid that if we rein in our runaway activity, we will become like train cars on a track that hit a wall—derailed and destroyed.

We vow not to stop. If we do, we will have to feel the pain of the past, the loneliness of the present, and the dread of the future. We will have to look at who we are, seeing our naked reflection staring back at us from too many memories and people of our past. We don't want to hear those stories echo through the canyon of caustic events in our personal history.

Stop the madness! I want to get off this futile Ferris wheel. I don't know who I am. I am drowning in a sea of activity. If I quit, I may get run over by the cacophony of current events that define my life. I won't be able to keep up, which spells failure in anyone's life dictionary. What if I get run over by failure or deceit? What if I see myself for the first time and don't like what I see?

Despite the preponderance of evidence to the contrary, people still believe that regular religious activities can assuage their inner turmoil and bring them lasting relief. Martin Luther rose up in the early 16th century admonishing the church faithful to go directly to God for communion, wisdom, and peace. The Apostle Paul urged the early Christians to be reconciled to God, to co-exist in harmony with Him.

But we continue, tossed about by every thought, some from without, yet still more from within. The latest image pushes us up the hill of the roller coaster. But when we get to the top, another point of view carries us down so fast that we feel out of control. Then up we go again, carried along on a wild ride until we reach the end, exhausted and barren. The fear still looms, but the thrill is gone. We thought we were going somewhere, but alas, in the end, we just hop off the ride with our hope hollowed out like a Halloween pumpkin. We are empty again, searching for another rush.

Once upon a time, I was on that ride. I came from a home that raged with dysfunction. It was easy to see and define the problems on the surface. But the inner turmoil was elusive and hard to pin down. Chaos ruled my heart, although I carried an exterior posture of control. Any peace I possessed was temporary. One day when I was in college, my dad asked, "Jean, what is your favorite word?" My Dad had a way of pulling things out of others by the questions he asked—thoughts and emotions that had not yet made landfall. He was bored with idle chit-chat. He wanted to engage intentionally with others, beyond the surface level. I replied, "Equanimity." That word just popped out of nowhere. I had recently come across that word in one of my college courses.

"Jean, what does that mean?" He asked. He had a great command of words, so he may have known the answer, but he was looking into my heart. I explained that it meant a mental calmness and balance deep on the inside—managing life with peace and composure that comes from deep within, come what may. The word comes from the Latin—"aequus" meaning level or equal and "animus" meaning soul or mind. When I put those Latin words together, I came up with peace, inner control, even-mindedness in the face of chaos, unable to be thrown off balance.

At once I wrote that word down on an obscure piece of paper and still have it tucked away like a special treasure. I have never forgotten that moment with my Dad or that word. I had always been searching for peace and balance. I was far from God, but somehow, I knew I had always been His. I did not realize that He had been carrying me all along the way toward serenity and composure. He would continue to shepherd me to green pastures.

Isaiah, a great prophet, once said, *You will keep in perfect peace those whose minds are steadfast, because they trust in You* (Isaiah 26:3, NIV). Our minds wander day and night, in and out down narrow pathways that lead to nowhere. God, through his Holy Spirit, wants to bring us back to center—to the truth, to purpose, to be all we were created to be.

Counselors and Life Coaches, through *Cognitive Therapy*, are teaching their clients to interrupt counterproductive beliefs and emotions, replacing them with thoughts that produce healthy responses to life events and harmonious relationships. Research shows that negative thinking gives rise to negative emotions. Negative beliefs and emotions create unhealthy bodies and relationships. Nonproductive thoughts yield unintended and undesired consequences. Productive thoughts give rise to clear minds, happy hearts, and powerful, proactive living. This book is designed to bring you back to center.

God has thoughts. His thoughts about you and toward you are infinite. He is concerned about what matters to you. You can position yourself to catch His thinking each day. You can corral your unbridled thoughts and put them in a holding pen. Your daily *Mindful Meditation* exercise will move you toward the unlimited thoughts of God. Holy Spirit wants to bring revelation to you each day. He will expand your heart and mind. Your body will become a regeneration station for the Holy Spirit to do His best work.

A mother hen broods over her unformed, unhatched chicks until new life appears. *First this: God created the Heavens and Earth—all you see, all you don't see. The earth was a soup of nothingness, a bottomless emptiness, a bottomless, emptiness, an inky blackness. God's Spirit brooded like a bird above the watery abyss* (Genesis 1:2, MSG). Everything was a mess. He will touch your troubled and wandering thoughts and put them back in order. After the Spirit of God moved across chaos, God began to speak. With each word a new spiritual and natural law was put in place, one day at a time. New life on earth began. Your heart will become His permanent home. His ideas and dreams will become a part of your being.

You will be immersed in His principles. As you become the new creature He designed you to be, you are now ready for the next step—reaching out to others, empowered by Mindful Meditation, spending time with your heavenly Father! You will touch others with the life of God within you! They will be attracted to the light of God in you and be changed by the hot coals of the Spirit you deposit in them.

Men in history, like Enoch, Noah, Abraham, David, and many others met regularly with God. They met face to face, heart to heart, and became God's friend. They heard His voice and helped others along the way. He and only He can tame the savage soul. He will build a strong foundation within. You are becoming robust and fit from the inside out—spirit, soul, and body.

Let's Define Mind

What is your mind? Where is it located? Is it my brain and all its chemical and electrical activities? Is it me and my brain just plays a part? I know where my brain is. It's in my head, and it seems to be saying something all the time. We have all heard the slang expression "talking head" meaning a person with an unyielding point of view whose talk is empty and pretentious. Or what about "talking off the top of his head" meaning saying whatever pops up in the brain without filters. Speaking out of your head would be a surface, factual, quick calculation, spitting out the details. Your brain is a marvelous creation. It takes in all outside and internal activities, sifts them through various categories, and stores them for you. Making meaning of all this incoming and stored perception involves more than chemical and electrical activity. It includes your mind.

When you were put together in your mother's womb, you became three essential parts—a spirit, a soul, and a body. Your brain is part of your body. When you die, your brain dies. One way people determine the point of death is when there is no more brain activity. Your soul is connected to the brain. Your soul acts as an eternal depository of the interpretation of all your life activities, past, present, and future. Your emotions and the way you think are there. You make decisions based on current input and the soul's interpretation and storage of information. While you are alive, your brain continues to take in information and helps your soul sift through and collate it all.

Your spirit is eternal. It was created by God, for God, to live inside your body to connect with Him. Your spirit stays attached to your soul and body while you are on earth. God designed your spirit to be the head or leader of your three-part being—spirit, soul, and body. When your spirit is united with Him, you are entirely alive. You even feel wholly alive as your soul responds to the life of God in you. Your body responds with good thoughts, God thoughts. Your body enjoys excellent health and healing as you think the thoughts of God. Your relationships become vibrant and more meaningful.

When you are touching God, your brain is entirely activated and can operate at peak capacity. It can be trained by your spirit as you begin to think God-thoughts. Sometimes your soul wants to be the boss. Its noisy emotions and opinions, based on truth or falsehood, want to be in control and make all your decisions, good or bad. Your soul and spirit are connected. God designed His word to be sharper than a two-edged sword able to divide spirit and soul issues that may be tangled together and secured with dirty duct tape. A two-edged sword can carefully cut both ways. It's a valuable, discriminating tool. The metaphor, double-edged sword means things can go both ways, having favorable or unfavorable consequences.

But God's Word is sharper. His Word, His sword separates the soul and spirit issues of your life. It gives you the mental space to bring your spirit to the front to be the leader. God's thoughts are alive and powerful. You are alive and life-giving when your spirit is in control and connected to God. You are powerful and able to run your own race. Instead of being double-minded, you are single-mindedly set to be persistent.

Finally, you can finish the race God has set before you. You are transformed by renewing your mind. You can indeed change your mind. Neuroscientists tell us that our brain's DNA and electrochemical currents are affected and shaped by how we think. As Jesus said, you become what you think.

What is Mindful Meditation?

Mindfulness has been practiced for centuries. Research shows that this method can reduce stress, improve cognition, reduce chronic pain, and improve sustained attention. Other studies show it can boost your body's immune response. It can also increase your resilience to the ups and downs of both internal and external stressors that may push you off center and cause you to respond emotionally in ways that are not profitable. Mindfulness has been used by counselors to improve relationships. It matters how you interact with others.

Mindfulness is defined as the practice of intentional, non-judgmental awareness of moment-to-moment experience. It is a mental break when you intentionally focus on the present moment without judging. You are shaping and focusing your internal attention on a particular thought. You say "no" to commentary mode. Those swirling opinions, comments, and analyses are tossed to the side. You are no longer at the mercy of your untamed mind. You are the director of your thinking. Being in the moment you play your own powerful part in the scene.

There is an energy that flows with awareness of the precious present. You are sifting through all thoughts and rejecting those that do not match your current intent or purpose. You are entirely alive and aware of what is going on in the here and now—good or bad. If it's dark, you fear no evil for God is with you. If it's good, you enter the experience with the fullness of His joy.

You are in control of your mind. We are to let the mind of Christ rule and reign. He was continually fully aware of who He was and His purpose. He was utterly present at each event and responded to every person with complete awareness of His mission. The practice of mindfulness is like taking your mind to the gym for a workout. As you practice, you will become steadier and more focused. You are directing your body and mind to stay in the present moment. You will be more productive at work, play, and relationships. Your body will respond to the life of God springing up in you. You can redirect your thoughts to become more wholesome, loving, and life-giving.

Mindfulness can be exercised when you are in a quiet, undistracted location or when you are with others. Put all preconceived thoughts on pause. In that stillness, God wants to speak. Your walls are down. You are standing in a field with no fences, no limitations. God foretold His plans for Jerusalem to Zechariah in Zechariah 2:1-5 (MSG):

> *I looked up and was surprised to see a man holding a tape measure in his hand. I said, What are you up to? I'm on my way, he said, to survey Jerusalem,*

to measure its width and length. Just then the Messenger-Angel on his way out met another angel coming in and said, Run! Tell the Surveyor, Jerusalem will burst its walls—bursting with people, bursting with animals and I'll be with her—God's Decree—a wall of fire around unwalled Jerusalem and a radiant presence within.

From this passage, God speaks to my heart like this, "My unwalled heart will be completely equipped with good things stocked by the Lord. The Lord will be a wall of fire around me, and He will maintain His fire of glory in my heart."

Walls have been erected around cities for centuries. They were primarily raised for defense—to keep the people on the inside safe from foreign invaders and to keep the enemy out. We have built thought walls to defend against hurtful invasion from others. Each time harmful things happen, we erect another thought wall or fortify the one that we previously established. We live life braced against adversity thinking "the bracing" will protect us. With our own hands, we build an inward frame of steel that will soon be destroyed by the storms of life. Will you join me in tearing down those "thought walls," and allowing God to protect and defend you? His fortification is life-giving. It will bring you peace and lead you down His path of overflowing abundance. Your thinking will become unclouded and focused.

Whether you are alone or with others, consider adding meditation to mindfulness. Meditation can be defined as intentional thinking focused on one thing. All other ideas or commentaries are pushed to the side as you ruminate on that one consideration. You are creating a mental hiatus where your mind is at rest. That's when God can speak. As a very young Christian, I began to have experiences where God would commune with me. At those times I would stop my mental activities and look up to God. He would speak from deep in my heart. Sometimes I would see things with my spiritual eyes. The visual display would be like a movie playing in my mind, and I would immediately know what God was saying. Sometimes I was sitting, quietly meditating on God and His word. Other times I was driving down the road.

I was alone with my heart fixed on Him. Other times when He spoke, I was taking a walk, taking a shower, or working at my desk. Another time I was alone, mentally preparing to speak at a major business meeting. I chose to let go of my thoughts and look to Him. I learned to interrupt my thoughts and let Him talk. Life can wait. Apply your mental brakes. God wants you to put Him first. When He begins to speak to your heart, don't get in a hurry. Allow Him to fully develop His thought through vision or a quiet heart-to-heart conversation. Write down what He is saying or what you are seeing. You may find as you develop this habit of Mindful

Meditation that He will speak more often. Sometimes when I know He wants to talk, I begin to write His words as they flow. His ideas are infinite, and sometimes they come faster than I can write. During this flow, His thoughts never really stop. I just quit writing. Don't forget—His ideas and insights are continually flowing toward you. They never end. You are always on His mind. He is eternally for you and never against you. God is love, and He gets great joy from speaking from His heart to yours about His great love for you.

I have always known that God wanted to speak with me. And I know He wants to express Himself to you too. Take a mental break and look up with all your heart! Allow your heart and mind to become a blazing fire of His glory. He wants you to be well deep in your spirit, soul, and body. His wellness will affect your physical and mental health. Your relationships will be mended and prosper. He will begin to lead you down His path where all authentic life exists.

Well Within—Let's Dig Deep!

Jesus said there is a well within all of us that should be springing up with His life. That life flow should be constant, pure, and eternal. It should flow continuously. This forward flow is dependent on your daily walk with Jesus through the circumstances of life. Even when the winds of life are contrary, He wants to walk with you. You can walk without Him or with Him. He wants to walk close to you like a friend. It matters who your friends are. Enoch walked with God. History tells us Enoch visited Heaven many times, spoke with God, and brought back messages to the people.

Abraham walked with God each day. He trusted what God said. *Abraham believed God, and it was credited to him as righteousness, and he was called God's friend* (James 2:23, NIV). Jesus said, *I call you my most intimate friends, for I reveal to you everything that I've heard from My Father* (John 15:15, TPT). He will speak to you as you walk close like a friend.

Paul visited heaven many times and was a powerful influence on everyone he met. One leader said about Paul that he was turning the known world upside down. Paul's visits to heaven and his daily walk with God fixed his heart and mind on mission and message. His strength and power were evident to all as he persisted through the emotional and physical pain. As you walk with God, your heavenly Father, each day, you are becoming His friend. He will reveal secrets to you. Jesus said that it matters what you are thinking and what you believe. As a man thinks in his heart, so he becomes.

You are what you think. You become what you think and what you hold on to! The natural man thinks the thoughts of a man. But the spirit of a man taps into the dreams of God and draws from the well of God within. Sometimes you must dig through the debris and rocks to get to the pure water of life that flows freely in your Well Within. Let's start digging. Let's go deeper!

Life is daily. Jesus taught us to pray "Give us this day our daily bread." God has thoughts of affirmation, comfort, and guidance flowing toward us every day. We must decide to tap into that spring of life flowing in us daily. We must think the thoughts of God until our own opinions are crowded out. Sometimes God shows us unproductive thought patterns that run deep and have clogged up our well for a long time.

Those ways of thinking have shouted over and over in our being and have formed grooves in the wall of our well so that the thoughts of God get trapped and crowded out. They are drowned out by the false truths we have believed. We must dig the deceptions out and cast them aside so that God's truth can flow freely and naturally.

False or fake truths may come from sources that surprise you. Sometimes our families have believed false truths for a long time—maybe for generations. Those false facts have become a part of us. They are hard to recognize. Everybody around you may think the same way and even speak those fake truths. Because others believe them, they appear to be true. You have heard them so long they have become a part of you. They seem like they are you.

Remember, as a man thinks in his heart so is he. You are what you think. For example, you may have heard "You are no good." "You will never learn." "You are a liar like your daddy." "Our family has always been poor." Or "There is no God. You must rely on yourself." "Too much religion will make you go crazy." "How could God love you? Look what you've done." "You've got to pull yourself up by your own bootstraps." Or "There is no such thing as sin. I can do what I want as long as I don't hurt anybody." Or "Our family is full of alcoholics, and I will probably become one." "My family is full of people who have cheated on their wives and husbands. If I get married, I'm sure to do the same thing." "Most marriages end in divorce. I'll never get married."

"Why would I want to know God? How could He be loving? From the beginning of time, a lot of evil has been committed against humanity in the name of God!" "My religion does not believe that." "I used to believe in God. When my mother got sick, I prayed to God that she would live, and she died. God is not real. And if He is, He doesn't love me anyway." Any of these assumptions sound familiar to you? You can probably add a few of your own to this list.

Cleaning up your well can be a daunting task, but, remember, life is daily. You can only live one day at a time, one moment at a time. Start digging today and purify your well. Allow God's thoughts to spring up from within you and overflow throughout your whole being—spirit, soul, and body.

You are becoming Well Within, Spirit, Soul, and Body! Let's dig deeper!

Each day God wants to talk to you. He wants to tell you who He is. He is your heavenly Father. He loves you with an everlasting love. He wants to tell you who you are. You are His creation, His son or daughter. He wants to whisper who others are when the wrapper is off. If you drop a piece of wrapped candy on the ground, it will look dirty and useless! But when you take the wrapper off, the candy looks, smells, and tastes just like it did before it got grungy. God does not see your dirty wrapper. He sees you as His loving creation, just as He made you. Sometimes those around us have been rejected, abused, and cast aside. Their lives have been struck by mayhem.

God does not see you or others with natural eyes. He sees with His spiritual eyes. He wants you to see as He sees. He does not decide how people are by what He sees on the outside. He looks inside and sees who He created them to be. He sees with His "possibility eyes," then He loves them and treats them as if they had already become what He sees—God's Possibility. He wants to give you those same "eyes of faith." Then you will be able to believe in His possibilities! You will be able to love with His "faith love," which is active and potent! It makes you treat others like your Heavenly Father would treat them and cherish them until they become the person God created them to be!

Take the Mindful Meditation Challenge! Each day you will be asked to listen to your Heavenly Father. He will teach you who He is. He will whisper how much He loves you and others. You will find renewed strength each day. You will become who God created you to be. You will find wisdom and power to help others become who God created them to be. Each day you will be challenged to see through Father's "possibility eyes." Let Father use you to help others understand who He is and who Father created them to be.

Through Mindful Meditation, you are becoming His Well Within: Uniting with the Heart of God!

Daily Call: Day 1

God calling you near: I am love and I want you near so you can feel My love and know My love. Nothing can separate you from My love. For I am love and I am in you. Take time today to separate yourself from all the details of your day and come apart to be a part of Me. Be quiet on the inside so when you are in a crowd, you will be centered on me and in my Love for I am Love. I want to speak to you about My love. My voice is still and small and I will speak inside you.

I want you to abide with Me and My Love. My love will refresh you like a cool drink of water on a hot day. Be still, get centered and meditate on My word, that is alive in you. Jesus said to the Father, *I have revealed to them who You are and I will continue to make You even more real to them, so that they may experience the same endless love that You have for me, for Your love will now live in them, even as I live in them* (John 17:26, TPT).

Write what the Father is telling you about His love.

_____
_____
_____
_____
_____

God sending you out: *Beloved, let us love and unselfishly seek the best for one another. For love is from God* (1 John 4:7, AMP). God will bring people across your path today. Some will be easy to love. Some will be hard to love. I challenge you to love each one. Love them with your eyes. Love them with your words. Love them with the small things you do for them, supporting them in their journey. Laugh with them. Cry with them. I will give you a confirming word for each. I want to use you to show My love. Name four things you can do today to express My love to others.

_____
_____
_____
_____
_____

Meditate on My words today: *There are three things that remain: faith, hope, and love—yet love is primary. So, above all else, let love be the beautiful prize for which you run* (1 Corinthians 13:13, TPT).

Daily Call: Day 2

God calling you near:

> *"Lord, You know everything there is to know about me. You perceive every movement of my heart and soul, and you understand my every thought before it even enters my mind You are so intimately aware of me. Lord, You read my heart like an open book and you know all the words I'm about to speak before I even start a sentence! You know every step I will take even before my journey begins. You've gone into my future to prepare the way, and in kindness, you follow behind me, to spare me from the harm of my past. With your hand of love upon my life, You impart a blessing to me"* (Psalm 139:1-5, TPT).

I am where you are. When you need me to hold you, I am there. When you need My counsel, I am there. I want to walk with you and talk with you as I once did with Adam and Eve in the Garden of Eden. You were made to be with Me, my Child. Come to Me when you are tired and weary, and I will give you rest. Breathe in the breath of life and I will give you My strength and My peace and My rest. I will give you My words of life. If your day seems dark, I will be the light for your path. Ask me and I will speak my words of life to you today.

Breathe in and let the Father give you words of comfort. Thank Him for being so close today. Express your thankfulness to Him here.

_____
_____
_____
_____
_____
_____

God sending you out:

"God, I invite Your searching gaze into my heart. Examine me through and through; find out everything that may be hidden within me. Put me to the test and sift through all my anxious cares. See if there is any path of pain I'm walking on, and lead me back to Your glorious, everlasting ways—the path that brings me back to You" (Psalm 139:23-24, TPT).

Lord, I want to walk in Your everlasting path. Purify my thoughts. Sometimes, contrary thinking grabs hold of me before I know it. I want Your thoughts to be My thoughts.

When things are dark today, I will lift my eyes and You will show me the light.

When I see people today who sit in darkness, You will give me a great light just for them. When they are tired and weary and can't break out of habits of sadness, hopelessness, and sin, You will give me light to brighten their path and get rid of the darkness forever. Show me how to bring Your light to a dark world. Father, show me those who are in darkness. You will give me words that shine as a light and make darkness run away.

Name two people you want to touch with the light and life of God today. Write here how you plan to be with them so God can use you to shine light in their lives.

_____
_____
_____
_____
_____

Meditate on My words today: *The one who always listens to Me will always live undisturbed in a heavenly peace. Free from fear, confident and courageous, you will rest unafraid and sheltered from the storms of life* (Proverbs 1:33, TPT).

Daily Call: Day 3

God calling you near: With deep love, I am praying for you. You belong to Me and My glory is revealed through your surrendered life.[1] Nothing can separate you from My love. I love you with an everlasting love. You have been tested and have returned to Me. You have been disappointed with life and you have come back to Me. You belong to me and will not be happy away from Me. I am in you and with you. You may go out, but you will always come back. I am your Father and I care for you! Life with Me is like a dance where you flow according to the music I give you. You flow out, but I always have your hand in Mine! You are close right now and I wrap you in My arms of love. I whisper My words of life in your heart right now. As we flow in the dance of life today, I have assignments for you. They are My plans. Follow My steps of life, light, and love.

Write here what I am saying. Let your pen flow as I speak My love to you.

_____
_____
_____
_____

_____

_____

God sending you out: Father, I hear You speaking Your words of life. I want to give Your life to people who are sick and dying inside. I want to speak Your words of life. You are the Resurrection and the Life. As I speak Your love today people will get up and live again. People will come close to you. People will know who You are and who they are in You. Christ, the anointing and the Anointed One is their hope of Glory. We want your kingdom to come to this earth. You are my King and I want you to be their King. Lord, take away everything that keeps me from you. Take away everything that keeps them from You.

Look into Heaven and write your assignment for the day.

_____

_____

_____

_____

_____

_____

Meditate on My word today: *Let My peace rule in your heart* (Colossians 3:15, NKJV).

Daily Call: Day 4

God calling you near: *What delight comes to those who follow My ways* (Psalm 1:1, TPT)! I made you like Me, with ears to hear. There are a lot of sounds coming into your ears every day. Some are loud. Some are soft. Some are kind. Some are harsh. Some accuse. Some excuse. Some are wise. Some are a waste. I designed your ears to hear and respond to My sound, My voice. Other voices cry out and say, "Pay attention to me." But I am opening your ears in a new way to hear My voice and another voice you will not follow. Put Me first today. Ask to know the True and Living God. Ask to hear My words of life. Delight in My words and meditate on them day and night. Take my word with you today. Your path will be lit up and you will know which way to go.

Write here what you hear Me saying about your path. Let My path and your path come together as you hear My words of life.

_____
_____
_____
_____
_____

God sending you out: Father, I hear you today. You are closer than ever. You have brought me near and I hear like never before. I am a tree planted by rivers of water. Even when drought is all around me, I can get a drink. I bear fruit each season. Apples, oranges, grapes, peaches, cherries, figs. I bear fruit year-round. My leaves never wither or fade. Whatever I do today will prosper.[1] I bear the fruit of God's Spirit—love, joy, peace, patience, kindness, goodness, faithfulness, gentleness, and self-control.[2] I feel You growing inside me. I am becoming a giant in faith and love. I am becoming like You, my Heavenly Father!

Surrender your life to Me again today. Let Me grow inside you and push all darkness away. Write your words of relinquishment to Me:

_____
_____
_____
_____
_____

Meditate on My words today: *Come closer to Me and I will come closer to you* (James 4:8, AMP).

Daily Call: Day 5

God calling you near: You may have been thirsty and dry and felt like I am far away. Today is a new day. I hear you calling to Me. Everything else you have called out to and tried has not worked. That's because you belong to Me. I hear you and I will not forsake you. Right now, I am opening up rivers in high places and fountains in the middle of the valleys. I am making your wilderness a pool of water. I am making your dry land springs of water.[1] Feel the waters rising. Feel the waters flowing over your dry and parched tongue. I am flowing in you and for you. Over and over My waters flow.

This wellspring of life will not dry up. Whenever you are thirsty and dry, I am there to quench your thirst. Better than the finest sparkling water, I bubble up within you. I am the pure water of life and you can drink freely. My water is living, and it is free. My springs never dry up.

What are you feeling as you drink from My fountains of living water. Write those feelings here:

_____
_____
_____
_____

_____

_____

God sending you out: Father, you have filled me up today. I go out with a well of water overflowing to the world. Everyone can see the fountain. They are drinking out of Your fountain. They all know that the Lord has done this and that God has created this fountain. They tell me their concerns and we go before the courts of Heaven together. You reveal the end and declare things to come. You are the same yesterday, today, and forever.

Father, I stand in the gap for Your people as you reveal Your Goodness and Your Mercy to each one. They belong to You. Your kingdom come, Your will be done in their lives. Others have said things will always be the same and they will never change. But You, Father, are changing the outcome. You alone are the Game-Changer. You declare the end from the beginning and from ancient times the things that are not yet done, saying, My counsel shall stand, and I will do all My pleasure.[2]

You are at a crossroads in your life. Write your destination, the destination God has planned for you. He will direct your steps and make your path straight.

_____

_____

_____
_____
_____
_____

Meditate on My word today: *I see you at the well. Ask Me for a drink and I will give you living water* (John 4:10, TPT).

Daily Call: Day 6

God calling you near: Today is My day. Today is your day. I have designed this day for you. You will shine. My light and My glory are rising on you. The world is dark, but you are My light. You are My city up on a hill in the middle of darkness. You can't be hidden. When people see the light, they are drawn to it. Push out of your expectations of this day, for I have plans that you don't yet know anything about. If I told you what I am going to do today, you would not believe it. For My grace and My mercy are overflowing in you, healing you and bringing health and healing to all you touch. You won't see all that I do. Some things will be hidden in the hearts of the people you touch. Come to Me so I can work My life and light in you for the world to see. Get up on the inside when you get up on the outside. Rise up! Shine! Your light has come. My glory is rising upon you![1]

What is God saying to you today about His life in you?

_____
_____
_____
_____
_____
_____

God sending you out: The Spirit of the Lord God is on me today. He has appointed me to represent Him in the world. I am His ambassador. I will be His representative. We will walk in harmony! The world wants to know God is real. God is real in me today. I take His love and carry His glory. I speak His words of kindness and affirmation to all I meet. I carry His good news. He has given His divine ability to bring good news to those in need. He is sending me to bind up the brokenhearted and to tell the captives that they are free. I will open their prison doors and tell them to walk out. This is the year of His favor. Today is His day, my day, their day.[2]

How can you bring His light to those who sit in a dark place? Picture where you are going today and who you will be meeting. What does God want to say to each one?

_____
_____
_____
_____
_____

Meditate on My words today: You are like a common clay jar that carries this glorious treasure within, so that the extraordinary overflow of power will be seen as God's, not yours.[3] You are holding My treasure in your earthly body.

When My light shines out of you, everybody can see that the excellent power that comes out of you is Me.

Daily Call: Day 7

God calling you near: Through My Son, everything was created, both in the heavenly realm and on the earth, all that is seen and all that is unseen. Every seat of power, the realm of government, principality, and authority—it was all created through Him and for His purpose.[1] Some of the barriers you see are places created by Jesus for Jesus, but the enemy of your soul is occupying that space and that place. I am saying "no way!" The enemy will not stand in the place I have prepared for you to occupy in freedom and in peace.

Shake off all thoughts that "you can't" and know that you can do all things through Christ who gives you strength and courage to fight for your own freedom and peace. Go in my power and tell the enemy he must go in Jesus' name. Bring the kingdom of God to the earth in the territory where you live. All power structures were created to be occupied by Jesus. He is the King of kings. He is the Lord of lords, You are a king and a lord. Take your place in the kingdom today. Be happy, for Jesus has overcome the world. His Kingdom is taking over. There is a new sheriff in town. Put on your badge of courage and honor. Drive the enemy out.

_____

_____

God sending you out: All the authority of the universe has been given to Jesus. He tells me to go in His authority.[2] Because all power in the heavenly realm and in the earth has been given to Jesus, I go and teach all people. I immerse them in the name of the Father and all His "Fatherness" means to them. I immerse them in the name of the Son and all the Son is. I immerse them in the name of the Holy Spirit and all the power, comfort, revelation, and guidance He brings to them. The words of Life will flow out of me like a river because I submit myself to My Heavenly Father and He takes me on a grand adventure. An exploit of miracles, both small and great. A venture filled with surprises.

What feats of fearlessness does your Father have planned for you today? Some are visible, and some are invisible. Ask Him to show you things about this day that you can only see with the eyes of your spirit. Ask Him to open the eyes of your spirit. Write what you see here.

_____

_____

Meditate on My word today: *Call to Me and I will answer you. I'll tell you marvelous and wondrous things that you could never figure out on your own* (Jeremiah 33:3, MSG).

Daily Call: Day 8

God calling you near: My truth-giving Spirit comes, and He unveils the reality of every truth within you. He won't speak His own message, but only what He hears from the Father, and He will reveal prophetically to you what is to come.[1] He will tell you all about Me and He will give you My strength. He will comfort you and He will guide you. You will need His comfort because My ways are not your ways. My ways are not the ways of this world.

You will need His comfort as I extract the lies from you as He leads you and guides you into all truth. You will need His comfort as you encounter troubles and heartaches. Even now you are troubled in your heart with the cares of this life. His comfort comes. Sometimes your heart aches because of the troubles you have caused. Sometimes your heart aches because of pain other people bring to you. Know that I am with you always. I'm with you on the mountain. I'm with you in the valley.

Sometimes your heart aches because you are in the valley of decision and the choices are not clear. Taking a stand sometimes leads to upheaval and heartache. Holy Spirit will lead you and show you things to come. When you see things to come, you can walk through the valley of decision and trust your future to Me. Put all your choices in My hands today. I want to make a way for you. I want to carry you through.

Write your choices here and let the Holy Spirit show you which way to go.

_____
_____
_____
_____
_____
_____

God sending you out: As you choose My way, I will give you My truth and I want you to be a farmer. I want you to sow seed in My harvest field. I will tell you what seed to sow. Right now I am getting the harvest field ready and ripe. You will reap a harvest. But right now, I want you to sow My seed. Some seed will fall out of your pocket because you are so full of My seeds of life you don't have room to hold it all.

Some seed you will plant intentionally in My field. Some won't produce, and you may get discouraged. Don't be disappointed by what did not happen. Look at the field that yielded the fruit that sprang up and kept on increasing. Some seed will fall into good, fertile soil, and it will grow and flourish until it produces more than a hundredfold harvest, a bumper crop. Listen with your heart.[2] My kingdom is ever-increasing, and I designed you to reap a harvest!

Where can you sow My word today? How can you sow it? Name some ways here.

_____
_____
_____
_____
_____
_____

Meditate on My word today: *I will perfect all that concerns you. My mercy endures forever. I will not forsake the works of My hands* (Psalm 138:8, NKJV).

Daily Call: Day 9

God calling you near. Child, listen with your spirit as I speak My word to you. You will be My minister in My sanctuary, a gatekeeper, and minister in the house.[1] I want you so close to Me. I want to bring you into My house to talk to you. I have chosen you to be My minister. You will stand before the people and minister to them. I bless you with ears to hear the voice of the Lord. I bless you will eyes that can see as I reveal Myself and My kingdom to you.

Your body is the temple of the Holy Spirit. Be filled with the fullness of God. Be filled with My glory. Let My kingdom come within you. Let My kingdom come upon you. Look now as I bring you into My temple, into My presence. The power of the Lord is so strong in My temple. Fall on your face and worship Me. Listen, Child. I am calling you to attention. Stand up on your feet. Hear me say, "Come up here!"

Get quiet and hear Him whisper. What is He saying to you in His temple?

_____
_____
_____
_____

God sending you out: I am giving you the grace to give up your own works. You have not chosen Me. I have chosen you. I brought you out of a dark place. I have chosen you and am fashioning you to walk into the future with hope and destiny. I have prepared a future just for you. I created you before the world was created and I designed your future. Surrender now all your own works and I will give you rest. I bless you with grace to allow me to lead you in the paths of righteousness because of My namesake, Jesus. Surely My goodness and My mercy will follow you all the days of your life and you will dwell in My house forever.[2]

What steps can you take today to be in His presence and walk His paths of righteousness? Write them here.

Meditate on My words today: *Lord, I praise you with every breath I take today* (Psalms 150:6, NKJV).

Daily Call: Day 10

God calling you near: My Child, just as you have allowed me to establish the Kingdom of God in your heart, I am sending you out to establish the Kingdom of God in your sphere of influence. Start first with your family. Come to me today with praise. Minister in my sanctuary. Minister to your family the way I minister to you. Minister in patience and lovingkindness. Let the Law of Kindness be in your mouth. Do not allow the unholy or the profane to be a part of our relationship or your atmosphere.

Be a minister in My house. Minister the cleansing blood and resurrection power of Jesus Christ to My people. Bring your family before me in the still of the night. Bring your family before Me before the day breaks. Speak My words of blessing. Speak My words of hope. *…pray at all times with all kinds of prayers and requests, in the Spirit, vigilantly and persistently for all God's people* (Ephesians 6:18, CJB).

_____
_____
_____
_____
_____

God sending you out: *My Child, ...as you go throughout the world, proclaim the good news to all creation* (Mark 16:15b, CJB). I bless you with a fervent heart of affection set on Me. I bless you with My glory that is much greater than all that you may suffer. I will provide a place for you among the people. I bless you with language to speak to your culture in words they understand. I bless you with the tongue of a ready writer, who translates the language of Heaven into the language of the people. You are My Lamb and I will give you everything you need for your journey. I am your shield and your great reward. I will provide a place for you among the people.

What can you do today to bring the Kingdom of God? Who does He want you to pray for? Who does He want you to speak to? Write it here.

_____
_____
_____
_____
_____
_____

Meditate on My words today: *My son, if you will receive My words and store my commandments inside you, paying attention to wisdom, inclining your mind toward understanding—yes, if you will call for insight and raise your voice for discernment, if* *you seek it as you would silver and search for it as for hidden treasure—then you will understand the fear of Adonai and find knowledge of God* (Proverbs 2:1-5, CJB). Father, I listen for Your wisdom and apply my heart to Your understanding. I cry out for Your knowledge and Your understanding like I am searching for silver and gold. Your treasure is hidden for me. I find Your reverence and knowledge.

Daily Call: Day 11

God calling you near: Sing, O barren, you who did not bear.[1] My Child, sing from the deepest part of you. Sing from where you are barren. Cry out loud. Let me hear your voice. Surrender to My call to the deepest part of you. I am crying out to touch that deep part... that part that is tucked away and hidden from tomorrow, locked up in yesterday. I came to heal you and make you whole. Did you forget who bought and paid for you? I bought you with the blood of My Son and I will not let you go limping along in life.

I will take you like clay and put you back on the potter's wheel and make you into My image. The storms of this life have distorted My image and I want it back. I will bring you through the storm to a fruitful land full of treasures. You will bring treasures out of darkness, diamonds you could not see when it was dark. But I am making all things new — a brand new heart I give you! You are my own creation and I love you with an everlasting love.

Write with a heart of thanksgiving to your Heavenly Father.

_____

_____

_____

_____

_____

_____

God sending you out: My Child, get ready to be fruitful as I send you out today. I'm not sending you out unprepared. Some of the treasures you have brought out of darkness are to share with a world covered in a shroud. *I will bless the thirsty land by sending streams of water. I will bless your descendants by giving them My Spirit* (Isaiah 44:3, CEV). The darkness in their lives is hiding their own uniqueness.

As you bring My love and good news to them, their eyes will light up as they see the gold in you. They will know they have treasures to bring out and sing about. Enlarge the possibilities in your mind. Look for the treasure. Don't be distracted by the dark. Look for the treasure without measure. Let's go mining for gold today.

What can you do today to bring someone out of darkness into His marvelous light? Write it here.

_____

_____

_____

_____

_____

_____

Meditate on My words today: *With great joy I draw water from the wells of salvation. I overflow with your gladness* (Isaiah 12:3, RSV).

Daily Call: Day 12

God calling you near: It's with lasting love that I'm tenderly caring for you.[1] My Child, get ready to be fruitful. I am painting a panorama of possibility that's big, that's large. Add some square-footage to your dwelling place. Abide with Me. Give Me room in your life. Disregard all thoughts of loss and disappointment. For your future will not be like your past. I am doing a new thing in your life and even you will see it with your eyes and touch it with your hands.

You will watch as I bring forth in the earth-realm the things I have prepared for you in heaven. The fruit of your womb will inherit the nations. I have given them to you as a part of your inheritance. For in your humility and surrender you are giving birth to new hope… a hope that was lost, but now is found… a hope that was small but now is huge… a hope that comes with no shame or loss, except the loss of your own dreams, that they may be replaced by Mine.

God sending you out: Father, bring forth in me surrender that leads to radical, bold trust in You. Father, when I am burning and being forged in the heat coming from the coals of fire, I am comforted knowing You are in control of its intensity. Let me surrender and stay on Your altar as You make me into Your image and Your likeness. Continue Your work even when it looks like the spoiler is destroying me. Change my image. Change my profile. Change what I am. I want to be like You.

Write what God is doing in your heart today.

_____
_____
_____
_____
_____
_____

Meditate on My words today: *Father, all the words from Your mouth are righteous. Nothing false or crooked is in them. Your wisdom is better than rubies. There is nothing I desire that compares with Your understanding. I long for Your knowledge* (Proverbs 8:8, CJB).

Daily Call: Day 13

God calling you near: My Child, I have searched you and know you better than you know yourself.[1] There is nothing about you that is hidden from Me. I know the things you thought were hidden. I know the pain you are afraid to share. I know the things you could find no voice for. I know the thing so deep, deep, deep. You see, deep calls to deep and I am in the depths of your heart. I am in the longing for loving and the desire for sharing.

I am in the hope-so's of your existence for I placed them in your heart. For your faith is the very substance of things that you hope for. Your faith is evidence that you believe what I say even when the "hope-so's" of life are not working out. Even when you can find no words for the "hope so's," I am there.

Write what some of your "hope so's" are. I want to fill your heart with My gift of faith to believe for the impossible.

_____
_____
_____
_____

_____

_____

God sending you out: Father, I thought I had hidden my thoughts and myself from You. When I looked I could not find myself and I could not find You. Now I realize I was hidden in plain sight—Your sight. Who was I fooling? You saw me all along, all alone. You were hidden from my sight by the cares of life, because of the road I chose. I could not find my way because it was not the way You chose for me.

I was not lost, just set aside for safekeeping. Thank you, Father, for sheltering me. I'm sorry for the road I chose. I'm sorry about the things I said. I'm sorry about the things I did when I thought I was hidden from Your sight. I wish I could take them back-just push rewind then erase. But You take them away and forget about them. You roll away the stone and give me a living, beating heart again.

Father is bringing a breakthrough to you. Write what He is saying to you.

_____

_____

_____

_____

_____

Meditate on My words today: *Father, out of Your favor You have had mercy on Me. I am so thankful to be among Your favorites* (Isaiah 60:10).

Daily Call: Day 14

God calling you near: My Child, I know you inside and out. I know every bone in your body. I know exactly how you were made, bit by bit, how you were sculpted from nothing into something. Like an open book, I watched you grow from conception to birth. All the stages of your life were spread out before Me. The days of your life were all prepared before you lived one day.[1] You are My workmanship. I created you in Christ Jesus before I laid the foundations of the world. You are My precious prize.

I am the potter and you are the clay. My works are marvelous—and that means you, too! I drew every part of you like a well-planned architectural drawing. I wrote your name and your days in My Book. I thought and think and will think about you constantly. Oh, that you would think about Me constantly. All the mathematicians in the world could not calculate the number of times I think about you. When you awakened to this life the day you were born and when you awaken to life each morning, I am with you.

Write what God is thinking about you. What was He thinking about you the day you were born? What does He think about you today? What will He be thinking in your tomorrow? He was there yesterday. He is here today. He is already there in your tomorrow.

_____
_____
_____
_____
_____
_____

God sending you out: My Father, teach me to love myself the way You love me. Teach me to value each part of myself because I was made by You and for You. Father, my heart is unclean. Search me and know every part of my heart. Put me on trial, not in Your courtroom of justice where the ruling could be unfavorable. Put me on trial in Your redemption room. Measure me with Your mercy and grace. See if there is any wicked way in me. Lead me in the everlasting way.

What is God revealing about your heart? Surrender it all to Him in His courtroom of mercy and grace. He wants to take what's bad and clean it up. He wants to take your best and make it better. He wants to turn you inside out and make you completely His.

_____
_____
_____

_____

_____

_____

Meditate on My words today: Never again will you be called "The Godforsaken Land" or the "Land That God Forgot." Your new name will be "The Land of God's Delight" and "The Bride," for I delight in you and I claim you as My own.[2] You bring Me joy. You are grafted into Me and you will be fruitful.

Daily Call: Day 15

God calling you near: Child, I see you when you sit down.[1] I see you when you rise up. I understood what you were thinking when you walked so far away. I placed you on the threshing floor to separate the wheat from the chaff. I placed a fence around you to keep you from going too far from Me. I placed a fence around you to keep out what you could not withstand. I placed my hand on you to discipline you. This knowledge is wonderful and high. This knowledge and love are hard to understand. You can't go anywhere that I am not. I am always there. You are always in My presence. You can't run away. If you go up to heaven, I am there. If you make your bed in hell, I am there. I sent my Son, Jesus, to save you to the uttermost! That's as deep and far-reaching as it gets. There is nothing deeper, wider, or higher than My love. I am there in the "uttermost's" of your life.

_____
_____
_____
_____
_____

God sending you out: Father, even when I fly away beyond the horizon, I feel Your hand leading me. Your right hand of authority and power is holding me up. When the darkness covers me, even the night is light around me. The darkness cannot hide from You. The night is shining like the day. Father, the darkness, and the light are both the same to You. You formed my inward parts. You knit me together in my mother's womb. You know my weakest parts and You know my strongest parts.

Surrender to Him again today. Surrender deeper. You were made by Him and chosen by Him. Write what He is saying to you today.

_____
_____
_____
_____
_____
_____

Meditate on My words today: Father, I will tell of the lovingkindness of God. I will praise You for all You have done. I will rejoice in Your great goodness. I will sing a song to You from my heart. The lively tune will overflow with praises of Your love, Your favorable acts, Your goodness, and Your mercies.[2]

Daily Call: Day 16

God calling you near: My Child, barbarians have invaded My inheritance. An army strong, organized, and effective, has attacked My land and your land, My heart and your heart, My home, and your home.[1] This army is from enemy nations and powers that seek to destroy you and everything that belongs to you. Your body is the temple of the Holy Spirit and they have polluted your temple, making what is holy unclean. They have entered the hearts of My people and are stealing life at will. The enemy is saying what is holy, set apart for Me, belongs to them. They are trying to take, and even now have in their hands, the people and things that belong to Me.

They are killing the body and soul of My people and feeding them to the birds of the air. The prince of the power of the air is directing their flight. He is stirring up their hunger and their thirst for more. The people and animals are coming, not to My ark of hope, but to feed on the dead remains of My called and chosen ones. This army has poured out the blood of My people all around the place of My Holy Habitation. No one is left to bury the dead.

Write what is happening in the news that shows you what the enemy of your soul is trying to do to God's people today.

_____
_____
_____
_____
_____

God sending you out: Father, I am Your called one, Your chosen from among these people who don't know You. You have chosen me in the furnace of affliction, out of the fire of adversity, and I will bear Your name to the nations. I will bear Your Light and Your Salvation. Even when I have wandered and wondered, You were there, You were always here with me. You said, "I AM!" Even now I hear You whispering words of hope and new dreams to a barren land. I hear You say, "I AM hope. I AM your dreams and none of them will go unfulfilled. Take My yoke on you and learn from Me." Father, today I look up and know I AM is here.

Write some things you can do today to stop the enemy and defend God's people.

_____
_____
_____
_____
_____

Meditate on My words today: *Be strong and of good courage. Do not be dismayed. For the Lord, your God is with you wherever you go* (Joshua 1:9, NKJV).

Daily Call: Day 17

God calling you near: The people who walk in darkness will see a great Light. The Light will shine on those who live in the dark land.[1] My child, friends and family are making jokes about you. They see My life in you and their darkness burns in them. They don't dare come near the light. Darkness is afraid of the light. It's afraid it will be exposed, put out, disappear, or be dispelled. They are right. They are afraid of your light. The enemy of their souls makes them run from your presence. They laugh and make fun of My goodness and My glory. But I am creating you to be their bridge to Me. I created them to be My light, My glory and My crown. You will lay yourself down and be that bridge as I reshape and rearrange you.

He is asking you to become a walkway to The Father. Are you willing to lay down your fear and your pride and be a bridge? Let Him know here.

_____

_____

_____

_____

_____

God sending you out: Father, Your Son made Himself of no reputation, so I will lay down in that low place. I will let go of the reputation that I thought I had and take Your Yoke upon me. For reputation comes from man, but legacy comes from You. I am building a family legacy that cannot be built by the hands of man. I will not build on a false foundation. You are leveling what I have built and raising up Your walls. No one will break in through the gates You build and steal anymore. You are sealing me in and sealing me away for Your purposes and no man will slap Your hands away. My heart is Your land and Your home. Even now You are writing on the tables of my heart. You are breaking the stony places and holding my new heart of flesh in Your hands. You are massaging it back to life—your CPR! I feel it beat with the rhythm of Your Love and Your Power.

Be still and let His Hands give you His CPR. Be still as He massages you to more abundant life, with His Power and His Glory. Don't hurry. Feel His touch. Write your words of surrender here.

_____
_____
_____
_____
_____
_____

Meditate on My words today: Peace I leave with you. My peace I give to you. I am depositing My peace in you today.[2] My peace is not like the shallow, fleeting peace you have found in the past. My river of peace safely carries cargo from port to port. My peace abides in you and steadies you through uncertain times.

Daily Call: Day 18

God calling you near: I am a sun and shield. I give grace and glory.[1] My child, I am not angry with you. My jealousy is burning for you, like fire. I want My people back. I created them and you for My glory. I created them and you to carry My glory. I want them. I want you. The fire you feel is not the fire of anger. Don't be afraid of the fire. My fire burns the chaff and sets the wheat aside. My fire stokes the kiln where you are heated to perfection and shaped to become My vessel of honor.

Ever wondered why you are attracted to the fire? You love to be close to the campfire. Your eyes are captured by the glow of My love and protection. The fire keeps the predators away. The fire keeps you warm when you are cold. The fire cooks your food when you are hungry. I am your fire of love. Come near the fire and let Me burn in your heart with My love. Be My sacrifice of praise. Be My sacrifice of honor. Be My sacrifice of glory.

Write your words of sacrifice to Your Heavenly Father here. Feel Him burn in your heart with His love.

_____

_____

God sending you out: Father, forgive me, Your child, for I have sinned and fallen short of Your glory. I want to see Your Kingdom come in my life. I stand in the place of those around me. Father, I confess my sins. I confess their sins. We have sinned and fallen short of Your glory. I want to carry Your glory. Why should the nations say, "Where is their God?" Let Your glory rise on me so others can see Your glory and see that You are real. Oh, restore us again.[2] Let them know You are alive. Cleanse me of all unrighteousness. Make me whole again. I bring the people before Your altar. Make us clean and holy, set apart for Your glory.

Write your words of surrender to His Fire and to His glory.

Mediate on My words today: Be diligent, aglow in the Spirit. Serve Me enthusiastically.³ Constantly rejoice in hope. Be steadfast and patient in distress. Be devoted to prayer. Continually seek wisdom, guidance, and strength. Contribute to the needs of God's people. Pursue the practice of hospitality. Like dry wood people are anxiously waiting to be ignited by the fire of My love.

Daily Call: Day 19

God calling you near: My Child, Heaven is My throne and the earth is My footstool.[1] I rule over all and am in all. How can you build a house for Me? I am looking for you. I am looking for a person with a spirit that longs for Me. Your body is My temple and I want to fill it. Listen for My word and be made alive again. Don't choose your own way today. Shake yourself, wake yourself, and choose Me all over again today. Put away your delusions, your fears, and hear Me. Didn't I promise to give birth to something great in your life? Do you think I have forgotten about the birth, the "something great?" I have not forgotten, and I will bring it to pass. Don't get tired of doing what is right in My sight. Wait on Me and I will bring it to pass.

What are you waiting for? What had God promised you? Write it here.

_____
_____
_____
_____
_____

God sending you out: My Child, I am extending peace to you like a river. I am comforting you like a mother comforts a child. I will show you signs and wonders. I am sending you into the world. For I so love the world that I gave My Son for the world. That love is burning in Me and flowing toward you and in you and swirling around you. I am sending you into the world, not to condemn the world, but to bring My Love and bring My Peace. I am pouring My Spirit out on all flesh. I am pouring My Spirit out on your sons, your daughters, your brothers, your sisters, your fathers, your mothers, your neighbors, your enemies, and your friends. Come to Me and get some of My glory and power to carry to all.

Take a step closer to your Heavenly Father. Get some of His glory and His power to carry to the world. What is your assignment from Heaven today?

_____
_____
_____
_____
_____

Meditate on My words today: Father, You put Your words in my mouth and they taste like honey. You give me a full meal of them.[2] You send me to people in my territory to speak Your word.

Daily Call: Day 20

God calling you near: My child, this is My covenant with you. The spirit I have placed upon you and the words I've given you to speak will not leave your mouth or the mouth of your children or the mouths of your grandchildren.[1] Submit yourself and your life to Me. I have plans for you. Turn away from your own will and your own ways to turn to Me. Live a life that honors Me in all you do. Call on Me with your whole heart. I have plans for you, to loose the bands of wickedness, to undo the heavy burdens, to let the oppressed go free.

I want you to give bread to those who are hungry, bring those who have no home into your house. When you see those who are naked, cover them with My Mercy, My Grace, My Glory. Just like Adam and Eve were naked and afraid after they sinned, you will meet those who are naked, yet they are clothed. They are afraid, and they don't know why. Cover them. Love them. Be My vessel of honor and power.

Write your words of love to your Heavenly Father.

_____
_____
_____

_____
_____
_____

God sending you out: My Father, I call on You and You answer me. I cry, and You say, "Here I am". I speak words of life to those who need You, and not words of accusation. I activate my soul to see those who are hungry, and I satisfy the longing of their soul with You. My light is rising out of obscurity. My darkness is turning to brightness like the noonday sun. Lord, You guide me continually. When I am thirsty, You give me a big drink of Your living water. I am becoming Your watered garden, Your spring of water that does not stop running. I submit my life to You. I am becoming well within.

Write your words of thankfulness to your Heavenly Father here.

_____
_____
_____
_____
_____
_____

Meditate on My words today: Lord, You are good. Your mercy and loving kindness are everlasting. Your faithfulness endures to all generations.[2]

Daily Call: Day 21

God calling you near: I am rich in mercy because of the great and wonderful love that I have for you.[1] My love for you is so wide, so deep, so high that you cannot measure it. It is more than you need and still more! Farther than to the moon and back. When you were outside My kingdom, you were spiritually dead, I made you alive together with Christ. When I raised Him up, I raised you up with Him. You are a new creation! Don't avoid me because you don't feel worthy of My love. Draw near to Me.

Tell me you have moved outside the boundaries I have set for you. I already know where you are. When I asked Adam, "Where are you?" in the Garden of Eden, I already knew. I just wanted Him to look and see where he was and tell Me about it. Come closer to Me and I will come closer to you with My forgiveness and love. I want to remove the darkness, turn you around, and light the pathway I have set before you! I welcome you with open arms.

Let His love and mercy wash over you. Tell Him where you are. Let Him tell you who you are and where He is taking you. He is whispering your God-potential into your heart.

Let Him tell you of His love and mercy. What path of light and life does He have for you? Write it here.

_____
_____
_____
_____
_____

God sending you out: Look for the God-potential in each person you see today. A smile often overshadows what God needs and wants to do in their heart. Share God's love with each person you meet—with your smile, with your touch, with your word. Let His smile, His touch, His word become your smile, your touch, your word. God with skin on! Allow God to use you. You will find God's love flowing in your heart. God's love is already in your heart—broadcast like seeds in a newly tilled field. He loves you SO much, SO you love others SO much! People will know you belong to Me because of your love!

Write My words of love for you and others here.

_____
_____
_____
_____

_____

_____

Meditate on My words today: This is how much I love the world—I gave My one and only unique Son as a gift. Now everyone who believes in Him will never perish but experience everlasting life. I love the whole world, including you and the people you will meet today!²

Daily Call: Day 22

God calling you near: I see you in your loneliness today. I see you in your heartache and disappointment. Life has not turned out just like you wanted. Look up. It's Me drawing you close. I have everlasting arms. My arms don't grow weak and tired from reaching for you. I want to hold you close today. Let me wrap you in My blanket of love. It's cold outside and there are many dangers. Let Me rescue you from your own thoughts. I created the sun to rule your day and the moon to rule your night. I have light to shine in your darkness. See how bright the dawn? Get out your sunglasses. You are going to need them. I have created today for you. Hear My tune rising deep in your heart? It's getting louder. You can whistle or hum it. It's a love song I wrote for you! Come up and away with Me. You are awesome and there is no imperfection in you. When you look into My eyes, you make My heart sing your love song. Don't look away. I want to sing a love song to you.

Write the words of love He is singing to you today.

_____
_____
_____
_____

_____

_____

God sending you out: Many lonely people surround you every day. Their hearts are longing for warmth and sunshine. Be their light today. Shine in their darkness. Often loneliness wears a smile. Look beyond the smiles today. The smiles are masking hidden works of darkness. Shine My light on everyone I bring close to you today. *So don't hide your light. Let it shine brightly before others so that the commendable things you do will shine as light upon them. Then they will give praise to your Father in Heaven* (Matthew 5:16, TPT).

List here the people you can shine on. How can you let My light shine through you today? This evening, write what happened as you shined brightly on each one.

_____
_____
_____
_____
_____

Meditate on My words today: *I am the world's light. No one who follows me stumbles around in the darkness. I provide plenty of light to live in* (John 8:12b, MSG). I am the light that illuminates and enlightens the whole world. Whoever follows Me will never walk a dark path without My light, My life, My wisdom, and My knowledge.

Daily Call: Day 23

God calling you near: I am making all things new in your life. You may be wearing the same clothes, living in the same house, eating the same food, working the same job, but I am renewing your heart. I make all things new again and again. You are discouraged because you don't see anything changing. I do my best work in the dark where man's eyes cannot see. When the day breaks you will begin to see My works of love. Change is in the air. When you look back, down, or around, you miss what I am doing. Look up! My life-change is coming near. Your life is hidden away with Me. Your life is not stalled. Your life is not on hold. I am holding all things in My hands and I am working My creative power in your life. All things are possible if you believe.

Be real with God today. What disappointments are you bearing? What works of darkness have stopped My life-flow in you? Write them here. Then look up! I am showing you things to come, things I am working in your heart and your life-circumstances. Write them here.

_____
_____
_____
_____

God sending you out: Other people are walking in discouragement today. They have lost the courage it takes to believe in Me and My possibilities. They want to feel alive again, but they are afraid to be disappointed. Fear of disappointment is a deep dark pit. Speak My words of courage to them. Bring revolution of thought and action to all around you. Pull them out of the ditch. Change the potential in the atmosphere. Speak My words of life today. Watch as they crawl out of the pit.

What words of life did I give to you? What words of life can you speak to others today? Write those words here. Never let them go.

Meditate on My words today: *Set your mind on things that are above, not on the things that are upon the earth* (Colossians 3:2, ASV). Set your mind on things above, where I live. Your life is hidden way up here with Me. Come up. With Me you are far above every work of darkness. Don't let fear, disappointment, and discouragement rob you today. Look up. I am coming near.

Daily Call: Day 24

God calling you near: All the treasures of wisdom and knowledge are hidden in Me.[1] The treasures are hidden for you. They are not for everyone. They are for treasure hunters who won't stop until they find My gold. If you are laboring on your own for success, for security, for peace, come to Me. I have already done the heavy lifting and the wisdom and knowledge are there for you to seek and find. Start your personal treasure hunt today. If you don't start, you won't finish. I will tell you each step to take. The way will not always be easy, but remember I am the way. I am always for you and never against you. Even when hard times come I will turn them into times of blessing. Just because you are having a hard time does not mean I am not with you. I am always with you. Just because things don't look like you expected, does not mean I am not blessing you. You are blessed and My favor rests on you.

Close your eyes and picture yourself as His favorite son or daughter. What would a loving Father say to His favorite child? What would a loving Father do for His favorite son or daughter? Don't be afraid to let your imagination go wild. He created your imagination. He produced your future before it happened. He knows the end from the beginning. See it unedited, say it unedited, and write it unedited here. Let your pen flow from His heart to yours.

_____
_____
_____
_____
_____
_____

God sending you out: I want to give with an open hand to all people. I don't deal with a slack hand. Who can you give to? What can you give and not expect anything in return?

List who you want to give to and what you want to give today. You are becoming a giver like Me. At the end of the day write their reaction. They will know that what came from your hand came from the Heavenly Father.

_____
_____
_____
_____
_____
_____

Meditate on My words today: *Do not be afraid and anxious, little flock, for it is your Father's good pleasure to give you the kingdom* (Luke 12:32, AMP). Sometimes you feel little because the storms of life are raging. Sometimes you feel little because I am so big. I want to be big in your life, so you will look to Me like a little child looks to his Heavenly Father. I am not a withholder. I freely give. I don't give grudgingly. I give joyfully! Receive from my hand, My child.

Daily Call: Day 25

God calling you near: *For if you love [only] those who love you, what reward do you have* (Matthew 5:46a, AMP)? People gather in groups with people like themselves. Others may be left out and rejected because they don't look like you or act like the group. I love all people and I have called you to love all people. Stop drawing lines between you and others that I did not draw. Jesus came and acted like Me. He showed you how I want you to be. He loved the lowly. He loved the powerful. He loved the needy. He loved those who were hiding their neediness. I am calling you near Me to be like Me. My way is not easy. You don't have many examples on earth. Judgment is my business, not yours. Take that critical look out of your eyes and look to Me. I will show you how to love like Me.

Close your eyes and picture yourself with love in your heart for all. Who have you judged not worthy of your relationship? Who have you judged not worthy of your glance? Who have you judged not worthy of your positive affirmation? Look deep into your heart. List those people here. Don't be afraid. Your Heavenly Father already knows who they are. He already knows your heart and He is longing to be a big part of it. Don't be afraid. Trust Him to take you places you have never been before.

_____
_____
_____
_____
_____

God sending you out: What can you do today to show love to people you may have rejected? List what you can do. List their reaction here. Write how hard or how easy it was for you to do.

_____
_____
_____
_____
_____

Meditate on My words today: Encourage and comfort and build up one another.[1] Lay all judgment aside and love one another. When you are wronged, don't plan to pay back. Paybacks are costly. Count the cost. Turn toward love. Turn toward acceptance. Turn toward Me and trust Me with the relationship and the outcome.

Daily Call: Day 26

God calling you near: Come now. Let's talk this over.[1] You have measured yourself against your own standards many times. You came up short. You compared yourself to others. What a mistake! You believed you had disappointed Me, yourself, and others. People may have given you a look that troubled your heart. But I have settled this matter already. Even though you felt like the black sheep of the family, I have already transformed you into a wooly lamb, white as snow. One of My names is "God, your Righteousness." I am the only one that can make and declare that you are righteous. I have already declared it and made the change. Twirl around. See? I have made all things new—even you. You are My creation, and nothing can reverse that metamorphosis.

Close your eyes. Use your imagination. I created it. Look at yourself. Now watch as I show you who you are—My creation, white as snow. Even now I am scrubbing you clean again. I am washing away all shame, all fear, all doubt. Your face is glowing. As you look into My eyes, My glory shines and reflects off your face like the moon reflects the light of the sun. I am your sunshine. Write about the transformation you see here. What did you see wash down the drain and go into the sea of forgetfulness? As I scrubbed you like a newborn baby, did you see the smile and glow come forth?

_____

_____

_____

_____

_____

_____

God sending you out: *Arise, shine; for your light has come! And the glory of the Lord is risen upon you. Darkness will cover many, but My light and life will rise on you* (Isaiah 60:1, NKJV). Many people will be attracted to the light. They will draw warmth and gather the courage to walk out of their darkness. Be intentional about all your relationships today. As you talk to each one, show them they are valued. As your light shines, each person will become like My gleaming, valued trophy. List each person here and their response to your look and words of affirmation.

_____

_____

_____

_____

_____

Meditate on My words today: *We couldn't be more sure of what we saw and heard—God's glory, God's voice. The prophetic word was confirmed to us. You'll do well to keep focusing on it. It's* *the one light you have in a dark time as you wait for the daybreak and the rising of the Morning Star in your hearts* (2 Peter 1:19, MSG). My sure word shines in dark places until dawn rises and the Son shines in the hearts of men. Speak My word and watch Me rise.

Daily Call: Day 27

God calling you near: The disciples went everywhere preaching, The Master working right with them, validating the message with indisputable evidence.[1] Go out and preach everywhere. I will work with you and confirm what you say with signs and miracles. People will wonder what happened. Let My words rise in your heart. My words are spirit and they are life. You can't see them, but they are an active force. Allow Me to take the words off the page of the Bible and speak them to you personally. As you meditate on My personal words, you will come alive. You will overflow with new life, sharing My active force with the ones I send you to.

Close your eyes. Use your imagination. Shut the world out and focus on Me. Allow Me to speak to your heart. You will hear Me in the stillness of your own heart. The voice will not be booming. It will be quiet. As you allow My words to bubble up unedited, they will come alive. Allow yourself to write what I am saying to you today. I may paint a picture. I may show you a movie. I may give you one word. I may give you a word from the Bible. It will be just for you. Write it here.

_____

_____

God sending you out: *Heal the sick, cleanse the leper, raise the dead, cast out demons. Freely you have received, freely give* (Matthew 10:8, NKJV). You have received freely, now give freely. "Miracle" is My middle name. I want to bring major shifts and changes in the lives of many. All things are possible for you if you believe. Choose one person to pray for today. I want to bring My life to many. Don't let fear hold you back. Write who you chose and write what happened here?

Meditate on My words today: Jesus said, God authorized and commanded Me to commission you. Go out and train everyone you meet, far and near, in this way of life, marking them by baptism in the threefold name: Father, Son, and Holy Spirit. Then instruct them in the practice of all I have commanded you. I will be with you as you do this, day after day until the end of the age.[2] Go and tell everyone all that I have done. Teach them My ways. Help them learn to follow Me. I am with you each day of your life, actively working with you.

Daily Call: Day 28

God calling you near: I hear your heart cry today and I am here to answer. I hear you say, "Help me, Father. Listen to me. Don't let me stay in this state of confusion. Deliver me and give me a way to escape. I want to dwell with You in Your strong tower on top of the mountain.

I put my hope and trust in You."

My child, put your faith and trust in Me when the waves on the shore are drawing you out into dangerous waters. There is no one like Me. I will lift you up like a helicopter on a life-flight mission. I will bless you and surround you with My healing comfort. Come away with Me, My love!

Write from your heart to your Heavenly Father about your imminent rescue and need for comfort.

_____
_____
_____
_____
_____

God sending you out: I am comforting you. Even now you know it. In the next little while, you will see it as your circumstances change. I am your shield and I am also your great reward. Even now you are ready to give My words of encouragement to others. Some are in fear and they need your courage. Some are walking through a dark valley and they need someone to walk beside them. Speak to them in their dark valley, and I will bring light to their path. Who will you speak to today?

What did you speak and what light did I bring through you to their situation? Write what happened here.

_____
_____
_____
_____
_____
_____

Meditate on My words today: *Oh God, you have taught me from my youth. And to this day I declare your wondrous works. Now also, when I am old and grayheaded. Oh God, do not forsake me, until I declare your strength to this generation, your power to everyone who is to come* (Psalm 71:17-18, NKJV). Even when you are old and have gray hair, I will not leave you nor forsake you. I want you to show My strength to this generation and My power to everyone you meet.

Daily Call: Day 29

God calling you near: Ho! Everyone who thirsts. Come to the waters. Hey. Listen. Pay attention. If you are thirsty, come to the waters. Don't have any money? Come anyway. Buy and eat. I have spiritual wine and milk. There is no price tag on it. Come on and buy without money.[1] Come closer. I am closer to you than your very breath. As you gently close your eyes, you can feel and hear each inhale and exhale. I am closer than that. I gave you your life and your breath. I breathed into you the breath of life and you became a living soul. Listen! You can hear Me breath My Hebrew, four-letter name, "Yod Heh Vav Heh" as you inhale—exhale. The old Semitic root word "hawah" meaning "to be" or "to become" gave rise to My name. The Romans wrote My name like this "YHWH". No one dared speak My name. Moses asked Me My name. My reply—I AM.

Today I challenge you "to be in Me". I have plans for you "to become" in Me. Turn on your personal media screen in your mind. What do you see yourself becoming? Don't be in a hurry. Let Me show you. Write what you see here.

_____
_____
_____

_____

_____

_____

God sending you out: As you abide in Me, your light will grow brighter. Your life flow is becoming life-giving. You have life to give to others. How can you give life to others today? Who will you seek out to give My life to? You are becoming like Me, a life-giver! Write here what happened today as you let My life flow to you, through you to others.

_____

_____

_____

_____

_____

Meditate on My words today: *For my thoughts are not your thoughts, nor are your ways My ways, says the Lord* (Isaiah 55:8, NKJV). *If you remain united with Me, and My words with you, then ask whatever you want, and it will happen for you* (John 15:7, CJB). Abide in Me. Let My words abide in you.

Daily Call: Day 30

God is calling you near: I am your hiding place and your shield. Hope in My word.[1] Wait for My word. Life is not always easy. Life is not always fair. Bad things happen to good people. The blunt blows of life make you want to hide. You can hide in Me. I have a hiding place of comfort, healing, and love. In My hiding place, I will surround you with the shield of My word. Connect with Me in your sorrow and your hurt. I will deliver My words of comfort straight to your heart.

Today crawl into My hiding place like a child playing hide-and-seek. *It is better to take refuge in the Lord than to trust in man* (Psalm 118:8, AMP). Turn on that multi-media screen I put inside you. What does My hiding place look like? What did I stock it with? What does it smell like? What kind of light do you see? What am I protecting you from? What does My protection feel like? Write it here. Take your time. Write it all down. There is much to show and tell.

_____
_____
_____
_____
_____
_____

God sending you out: *It was good for me that I have been afflicted, that I may learn Your statutes* (Psalm 119:71, AMP). My child, it was good that you had hard times. You felt like your life was coming apart at the seams and you were coming unraveled. You have come apart to be a part of Me. I will hide you until the day of your coming out party. You will come out like a new person. I AM the same yesterday, today, and forever. I AM the beginning. I AM the end. I know your beginning and I know your end. Let me give you a glimpse of your future here. Write what you see.

_____
_____
_____
_____
_____
_____

Meditate on My words today: *How sweet are Your words to my taste, sweeter than honey to my mouth* (Psalm 119:103, AMP)! I want to hear Your voice in my heart and in my head. I don't want to be disconnected from You. Tether my heart to Your Word. You will never leave me. You will never forsake me.

NOTES

Day 3
1. John 17:9-10 KJV

Day 4
1. Psalm 1:3 RSV
2. Galatians 5:22-23 RSV

Day 5
1. Isaiah 41:17-18 KJV
2. Isaiah 46:10 KJV

Day 6
1. Isaiah 60:1 NKJV
2. Isaiah 61:1-2 AMP
3. 2 Corinthians 4:7 TPT

Day 7
1. Colossians 1:16 TPT
2. Matthew 28:18-19 TPT

Day 8
1. John 16:13 TPT
2. Luke 8:8 TPT

Day 9
1. Ezekiel 44:11 NKJV
2. Psalm 23:6 NKJV

Day 11
1. Isaiah 54:1a ASV

Day 12
1. Isaiah 54:11-12, 14 KJV

Day 13
1. Psalm 139:1 AMP

Day 14
1. Psalm 139:16 MSG
2. Isaiah 62:4 TLB

Day 15
1. Psalm 139:2 TLB
2. Isaiah 63:7 KJV

Day 16
1. Psalm 79: 1 TPT

Day 17
1. Isaiah 9:2 AMP
2. John 14:27 NKJV

Day 18
1. Psalm 84:11 NKJV
2. Isaiah 60:1 NKJV
3. Romans 12:11 AMP

Day 19
1. Isaiah 66:1 AMP
2. Ezekiel 3:2-3 MSG

Day 20
1. Isaiah 59:21 MSG
2. Psalm 100:5 AMP

Day 21
1. Ephesians 2:4 AMP
2. John 3:16 TPT

Day 24
1. Colossians 2:3 CJB

Day 25
1. 1 Thessalonians 5:11 AMP

Day 26
1. Isaiah 1:18 KJV

Day 27
1. Mark 16:20 MSG
2. Matthew 28:18-20 MSG

Day 29
1. Isaiah 55:1 NKJV

Day 30
1. Psalm 119:114 CJB

ABOUT THE AUTHOR

Jeanie would welcome an opportunity to speak to your group. Her wealth of knowledge, based on her own experience, includes:

- How to Touch the Heart of God and Hear His Voice
- Creating Wellness Within: Decreasing Your Toxic Load– Spirit, Soul, and Body
- Think You Have a Book in You? Getting Started 101\
- Cancer Diagnosis: Facing the Giants

Contact Jeanie at: jeanie.winebarger@gmail.com

Jeanie Winebarger
903-705-2755

www.ingramcontent.com/pod-product-compliance
Lightning Source LLC
Chambersburg PA
CBHW052058070526
44584CB00017B/2234